365
Reflections on
DAUGHTERS

Also available from Adams Media Corporation

365
Reflections on
DAUGHTERS

Selected and arranged by
Dahlia Porter and Gabriel Cervantes

Adams Media Corporation
Holbrook, Massachusetts

Published by Adams Media Corporation
260 Center Street, Holbrook, MA 02343

ISBN: 1-55850-812-0

Printed in Canada.
J I H G F E D C B

Library of Congress Cataloging-in-Publication Data
365 reflections on daughters : edited by Dahlia Porter and Gabriel Cervantes.
        p.   cm.
Includes bibliographical references.
ISBN 1–55850–812–0 (paperback)
1. Daughters—Quotations, maxims, etc. I. Porter, Dahlia. II. Cervantes, Gabriel.
        PN6084.D37A15   1997
306.874—dc21   97–27066
                                CIP

This book is available at quantity discounts for bulk purchases.
For information, call 1-800-872-5627 (in Massachusetts, 781-767-8100).

Visit our home page at http://www.adamsmedia.com

For Helen and Richard
with love

Contents

❧

My Daughter / 1

A Mother . . . / 69

. . . and a Father / 129

Parents / 181

The Family Face / 207

The Root of the Heart / 245

Life / 295

Words of Wisdom / 339

My

Daughter

*Y*our happiness was my first wish, and the pursuit of all my actions, divested of all self-interest. So far I think you ought, and believe you do, remember me as your real friend.

—*Lady Mary Whortey Montagu,
in a letter to her daughter*

$\mathcal{I}$ have so many anxieties about her growing up. I just hope she will get a chance to grow up. I hope there's a world for her to grow up in. I watch the news and I think, " . . . they're going to blow up the world, just when I've got this little peach here."

Meryl Streep, of her daughter

*H*ad I only known
My longing
would be so great,
Like a clear mirror
I'd have looked on you —
Not missing a day,
Not even an hour.

—Otomo No Sakanoe,
to her eldest daughter

$\mathcal{I}$ never thought she'd turn on me. When I was sinking in a sea of diapers, formulas and congenital spitting, Mother couldn't wait to pull her grandchildren onto her lap and say, "Let me tell you how rotten your mommy was. She never took naps, and she never picked up her room, and she had a mouth like a drunken sailor in Shanghai. I washed her mouth out with soap so many times I finally had to starch her tongue."

—*Erma Bombeck*

*T*hings change so fast. You can't use 1971 ethics on someone born in 1971. Whatever she does is going to look far-out to me. I hope I'll either like it or keep my mouth shut.

— *Grace Slick,*
of her daughter as an infant

There was a little girl,
Who had a little curl
Right in the middle of her forehead;
And when she was good
She was very, very good,
And when she was bad she was horrid.

—*Henry Wadsworth Longfellow*

I've allowed you to nourish me as I've nourished you. I've allowed that bond between mother and daughter to gradually grow, to reach beyond the limits I've always held. Not that I didn't love your brothers and sisters . . . but with your birth, the child I didn't want but at last proved my worth so that I could say, Enough, I myself began to bloom.

—*Elaine Marcus Starkman,*
to her daughter

$\mathcal{T}$hy daughters dright thy walks
adorn,
Gay as the gilded summer sky,
Sweet as the dewy, milk-white thorn,
Dear as the raptured thrill of joy.

— *Robert Burns*

$\mathcal{O}$ur child will not be raised in tissue paper! We don't even want her to hear the word "princess."

—*Juliana, queen of the Netherlands,*
of her daughter

I shall be glad to see thee back, daughter, for I miss thee dreadfully. I wish I did not! I was taking a nap in my chair today, and I thought I heard thee rustling thy papers, and I looked over at thy table expecting to see thee, and alas! Thee was not there, and it was dreadful.

—*Hannah Whitall Smith*

$\mathcal{W}$e are together, my child and I. Mother and child, yes, but *sisters* really, against whatever denies us all that we are.

—*Alice Walker,*
of her daughter

*W*hat can I say, but that it's not
easy?
I cannot lift the stones out of your way,
And I can't cry your bitter tears for you.
I would if I could, what can I say?
. . . But we're not one, we're worlds
apart.
You and I,
Child of my body, bone of my bone,
Apple of my eye.

—*Rosalie Sorrels*

$\mathcal{J}$ only have two rules for my newly born daughter: she will dress well and never have sex.

—*John Malkovich*

There be none of beauty's
daughters
With a magic like thee;
And like music on the waters
Is thy sweet voice to be.

—*Lord Byron*

When I held you, Jane—my
first baby—in my arms, I
had the greatest thrill I have ever
experienced.

—*Mrs. Colbert,*
to her daughter

*E*very woman endeavors to breed
her daughter a fine lady,
qualifying her for her station in which
she will never appear, and at the same
time incapacitating her for that
retirement to which she is destined.
Learning, if she has a real taste for it,
will not only make her contented, but
happy in it.

—*Lady Mary Whortley Montagu,*
in a letter to her daughter

*W*hat seas what shores what
gray rocks and what
islands
What water lapping the bow
And scent of pine and the woodthrush
singing through the fog
What images return
O my daughter.

— *T.S. Eliot*

There is so much between us, sad and good. I find you a fascinating person. So there is much more than mother-daughter love. You really do enrich my life and teach me.

—Nan Hunt,
in a letter to her daughter Diana

I looked at my daughters, and my boyhood picture, and appreciated the gift of parenthood, at that moment, more than any other gift I have ever been given. . . . Who else would think your insignificant and petty life so precious in the living, so rich in its expressiveness, that it would be worth partaking of what you were, to understand what you are?

—*Gerald Early*

$\mathcal{I}$ was so proud of you and thrilled at having you so close to me on our long walk in Westminster Abbey, but when I handed your hand to the Archbishop I felt that I had lost something very precious.

—*King George VI of England,*
of his daughter Elizabeth on her wedding day

*A*nd I will whisper blithely
in your dreams
when you are as old as I
my hard time over.
Meanwhile, keep warm
your love, your bed
and your wise heart and head
my good daughter.

— *Carolyn Kizer*

$\mathcal{I}$ hate poverty and Dirt and here I
shall have to live in such in my
last days. Don't pity me Janey. Forgive
all my faults and the wrong I have done
you.

—*Calamity Jane,*
in a journal to her daughter

What I would like to give my daughter is freedom. And this is given by example, not by exhortation. Freedom is a loose leash, a license to be different from your mother and still be loved. . . . Freedom is . . . not insisting that your daughter share your limitations. Freedom also means letting your daughter reject you when she needs to and come back when she needs to. Freedom is unconditional love.

—*Erica Jong*

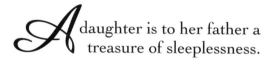

A daughter is to her father a treasure of sleeplessness.

—*Ben Siva*

Seeing you sleeping peacefully on your back among your stuffed ducks, bears and basset hounds would remind me that no matter how good the next day might be, certain moments were gone forever . . .

—*Joan Baez*

*W*ho can describe the transports of a heart truly parental on beholding a daughter shoot up like some fair and modest flower, and acquire, day after day, fresh beauty and growing sweetness, so as to fill every eye with pleasure and every heart with admiration.

—*James Fordyce*

*M*y face is a caricature of hers and her soul is a caricature of mine. In fact, she has no soul. She is my substance. She robbed me of substance in the womb. That's why I named her Narcissa. . . . She grew her beauty on me like a flower on a dunghill. She is my material. I am her soul. We are that perilous pair.

—*Rose O'Neill*

And then last night I tiptoed up
  To my daughter's room and
                heard her
Talking to someone, and when I opened
The door, there was no one there . . .
Only she on her knees, peeking into
          Her own clasped hands.

—*Amiri Baraka*

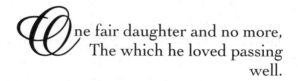

One fair daughter and no more,
The which he loved passing
well.

— *William Shakespeare*

*I*t is clear to me, every little while, that my soul is not big enough to get along without a very personal reason for existence. You will be that person for a long, *long* time yet. Won't you?

—*Crystal Eastman,*
in a letter to her mother Annis Ford Eastman

$\mathcal{W}$e *need* each other. I'm glad the tho't of me so often helps you—it is because I am not too near— you forget my fatal weakness and only know my love and my aching desire to be *with you where you are* in all the heights and depths.

—*Annis Ford Eastman,*
in a letter to her daughter Crystal

$\mathcal{M}$y ten-year-old daughter is my
#1 power source.

—*Hanan Mikhail Ashrawi*

$\mathcal{B}$efore you were conceived I
wanted you
Before you were born I loved you
Before you were here an hour I would
die for you
This is the miracle of life.

—*Maureen Hawkins*

$\mathcal{M}$any daughters have done
virtuously, but thou
excellest them all.
Favor is deceitful, and beauty is vain:
but a woman that feareth the lord, she
shall be praised.
Give her the fruit of her hands; and let
her own works praise her in the gates.

The Holy Bible,
Proverbs 31:29–31

$\mathcal{C}$harles . . . looked upon the poor little red thing and blurted, "She's more beautiful than the Brooklyn Bridge."

—Helen Hayes,
of their infant daughter

$\mathscr{P}$rince, I warn you, under the rose,
   Time is the thief you cannot banish.
These are my daughters I suppose.
But where in the world did the children
                                    vanish?

—*Phyllis McGinley*

$\mathcal{I}$n giving our daughter life, her father and I had also given her death, something I hadn't realized until the new creature flailed her arms in what was now infinite space. We had given her disease and speeding cars and flying cornices: once out of the fortress that had been myself, she would never be safe again . . . And until the day we die we fear the phone that rings in the middle of the night.

—*Mary Cantwell*

$\mathcal{M}$aria and I are much alike . . .
to love her requires me to
love myself.

—*Anna Quindlen,*
of her daughter

*P*ainting is an emancipation for young girls; it gives them the right to look men in the face and in detail. Admiration purifies everything. If I had a daughter, she should paint landscapes.

—*Mme. de Girardin*

$\mathcal{T}$hou art thy mother's glass, and
she in thee
Calls back the lovely April of her prime.

— *William Shakespeare*

*S*o I want to tell you now, for you to remember then (in case I don't get another moment like this in the next twenty years) that I love you devotedly . . . that I admire you for your struggles to mature and liberate yourself; that I respect your intellect; that I am proud to have had a hand in your upbringing; that I hope we shall be friends as long as I live.

—*Joan Scott, to her daughter Ann*

*B*rushing out my daughter's dark
silken hair before the mirror
I see the grey gleaming on my head,
the silver-haired servant behind her. Why is it
just as we begin to go
they begin to arrive . . .

— *Sharon Olds*

I long to put the experience of fifty years into your young lives, to give you at once the key to that treasure chamber every gem of which has cost me tears and struggles and prayers, but you must work for these inward treasures yourselves.

—*Harriet Beecher Stowe,*
to her daughters

*T*hree years she grew in the sun
and shower,
Then Nature said, 'A lovelier flower
On earth was never sown;
This Child I to myself will take;
She shall be mine, and I will make,
A Lady of my own.'

— *William Wordsworth*

When she comes and looks in
my face and calls me
"mother," indeed I then truly am a
mother . . .

—*Emma Hamilton*

*W*hile the pre-adoption seemed extra-ordinary, your life with me seems ordinary, in the sense that you are my daughter and I am your mother and the fact of adoption is no longer relevant. . . . Our ties seem so deep, coming from some faraway dark womblike place, that they can be no different nor less than those of the biological parent.

—*Nan Bauer Maglin,*
to her adopted daughter Quintana

I never liked your manner towarde me better than when you kissed me laste for I loue when daughterly loue and deere charitie hathe laisor to looke to worldly curtesye. Fare well my deere childe and praye for me, and I shall for you and all your friendes that we maie merily meete in heaven.

— *Thomas More,*
in a last letter to his daughter Margaret on the
night prior to his execution

$\mathcal{H}$e who has daughters is always
a shepherd.

—*Anonymous*

I don't mind owning that I wished for a daughter. I can't help thinking she would have resembled me more and would have been perhaps easier to understand. This is a selfish feeling, I admit; but boy or girl, they are very interesting and infinitely touching.

—*Joseph Conrad*

*R*umble my bellyful. Spit, fire,
spout, rain.
Nor rain, wind, thunder, fire, are my
daughters.
I tax not you, you elements, with
unkindness.

— *William Shakespeare*

To my daughter Leonora without
whose never-failing sympathy
and encouragement this book would
have been finished in half the time.

—*P. G. Wodehouse,*
in the dedication to The Heart of a Goof

*M*y love for you shall accompany you your whole life long—I kiss you—and all who are kind to you. Farewell, my dear—thinking of you to the end with greatest love.

—*Rose Schlösinger,*
in a last letter to her daughter prior to her execution
for her participation in the underground movement
in Nazi Germany

he thoughts of a *daughter* are a
kind of memorial.

—*Enid Bagnold*

*W*hen my daughter looks at me,
she sees a small old lady.
That is because she sees only with her
outside eyes. She has no *chuming;* she
would see a tiger lady. She would have
careful fear. . . .

—*Amy Tan*

*D*aughter, take this amulet
tie it with a cord and
caring
I'll make you a chain of coral and pearl
to glow on your neck. I'll dress you nobly.
A gold clasp too—fine, without flaw
to keep you always.

—*Mwana Kupona Msham*

*M*any a man wishes he were
strong enough to tear a
telephone book in half—especially if he
has a teenage daughter.

— *Guy Lombardo*

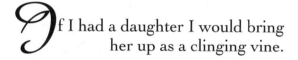

If I had a daughter I would bring her up as a clinging vine.

—*Mary Lathrop*

*A*nd you my daughter
who I will not
know —
I feel in mine
your small, hot hand,
I see your green eyes
lighting already
with my mother's faraway look,
and the kisses . . .
from my lover's warm, dark lips
smiling from yours —
made for kisses.

—*Mary Dorcey*

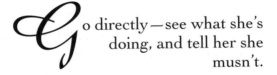

*G*o directly — see what she's doing, and tell her she musn't.

—Punch

$\mathcal{M}$other may I go to bathe?
Yes my darling
daughter.
Hang your clothes on yonder tree,
But don't go near the water.

—*Nursery rhyme*

hen farewell, my dear; my loved
daughter, adieu;
The last pang of life is in parting
from you.

— *Thomas Jefferson*

*L*ew Fields: Ladies don't write lyrics.
Dorothy Fields: I'm no lady, I'm your daughter.

—*Dorothy Fields*

I felt something impossible for me to explain in words. Then when they took her away, it hit me. I got scared all over again and began to feel giddy. Then it came to me — I was a father.

—*Nat King Cole,*
on the birth of his first child, Natalie

Thus far my daughter has understood very clearly that the best part of her life would be that which she spent in allowing herself to be courted, and she did not feel in haste to become the servant of one man, when she can command several. Therefore, so long as the game pleases her, she can amuse herself; but if you pleasure her better than the game, the game can cease.

—*George Sand*

Oh my son's my son till he gets
him a wife,
But my daughter's my daughter all her
life.

—*Dinah Mulock Craik*

A daughter is a companion, the friend, and confidant of her mother, and the object of a pleasure something like love between the angels to her father.

—*Richard Steele*

A

Mother . . .

$\mathcal{M}$y mother is everywhere . . .
In the perfume of a rose,
The eyes of a tiger,
The pages of a book,
The food that we partake,
The whistling wind of the desert,
The blazing gems of sunset,
The crystal light of full moon,
The opal veils of sunrise.

—*Grace Seton-Thompson*

[*M*y Dearest Mother] Ah! what a joy is it to be able to turn in full confidence to the one whom we have to thank for our existence.

—*Frederika Bremer,*
in a letter to her mother

$\mathcal{I}$ look at my hands, Momma
And I see yours
And those of your mother before you.

—*Laura Davis*

I really must venture to tell you, dear Maman, that you have very little idea what I am really like. It is a long time now since we lived together and you often forget I am now twenty-seven years old and that my character was bound to undergo many changes since I was quite a girl.

—George Sand,
in a letter to her mother

$\mathcal{M}$y mother is a poem I'll never
be able to write
though everything I write is a poem to
my mother.

—*Sharon Doubiago*

$\mathcal{P}$erhaps you still don't realize . . . how very much I have admired you: for your work, your teaching, your strength and your creation of our exquisite home . . . I don't think I've ever specifically told you all that I love and revere, and it is a great, great deal!

—*Sylvia Plath,*
in a letter to her mother

I knew what I had to have before my soul would rest. I wanted to belong — to belong to my mother. And in return — I wanted my mother to belong to me.

— *Gloria Vanderbilt*

I love my mother for all the times she said absolutely nothing. . . . Thinking back on it all, it must have been the most difficult part of mothering she ever had to do: knowing the outcome, yet feeling she had no right to keep me from charting my own path. I thank her for all her virtues, but mostly for never once having said, "I told you so."

—*Erma Bombeck*

My mother, religious-negro,
proud of
having waded through a storm, is very
obviously,
a sturdy Black bridge that I
crossed over, on.

— Carolyn M. Rodgers

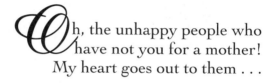

$\mathcal{O}$h, the unhappy people who have not you for a mother! My heart goes out to them . . .

— *Crystal Eastman,*
in a letter to her mother, Annis Ford Eastman

*M*ost of all the other beautiful
things in life come by twos
and threes, by dozens and hundreds.
Plenty of roses, stars, sunsets, rainbows,
brothers and sisters, aunts and cousins,
comrades and friends—but only one
mother in the whole world.

—*Kate Douglass Wiggin*

$\mathcal{M}$y mother wasn't what the world would call a good woman. She never said she was. And many people, including the police, said she was a bad woman. But she never agreed with them, and she had a way of lifting up her head when she talked back to them that made me know she was right.

— *Boxcar Bertha*

I had the most satisfactory of childhoods because Mother, small, delicate-boned, witty, and articulate, turned out to be exactly my age.

—*Kay Boyle*

To her whose heart is my heart's
quiet home,
To my first Love, my Mother, on whose
knee
I learnt love-lore that is not
troublesome.

—*Christina Rossetti*

*W*hatever beauty or poetry is to be found in my little book is owing to your interest in and encouragement of all my efforts from the first to the last; and if ever I do anything to be proud of, my greatest happiness will be that I can thank you for that, as I may do for all the good there is in me; and I shall be content to write if it gives you pleasure.

—*Louisa May Alcott,*
in a letter to her mother

$\mathcal{P}$lease judge anyone who criticizes me for it [her relationship with her husband] with the head and the heart of a mother, for both ought to be on my side.

— *George Sand,*
in a letter to her mother

$\mathcal{M}$y mother and I could always
look out the same window
without ever seeing the same thing.

—*Gloria Swanson*

When the strongest words for what I have to offer come out of me sounding like words I remember from my mother's mouth, then I either have to reassess the meaning of everything I have to say now, or re-examine the worth of her old words.

—*Audre Lorde*

$\mathcal{I}$ discovered as I wrote . . . a
woman who kept her
deepest feelings, her most profound
sorrows, sealed from my view . . .
invariably acts out of love.

—*Margaret Truman,*
in the forward to her biography of her mother

How simple a thing it seems to
me that to know ourselves
as we are, we must know our
mother's names.

—*Alice Walker*

$\mathcal{N}$ow that I am in my forties, she tells me I'm beautiful . . . and we have the long, personal and even remarkably honest phone calls I always wanted so intensely I forbade myself to imagine them. . . . Perhaps Shaw was correct and if we lived to be several hundred years old, we would finally work it all out. I am deeply grateful. With my poems, I finally won even my mother. The longest wooing of my life.

— *Marge Piercy*

Who ran to help me when I fell,
And would some pretty
story tell,
Or kiss the place to make it well?
My mother.

—*Ann Taylor*

To describe my mother would be
to write about a hurricane in
its perfect power.

—*Maya Angelou*

$\mathcal{M}$y mother wanted me to be her wings, to fly as she never quite had the courage to do. I love her for that. I love the fact that she wanted to give birth to her own wings.

—*Erica Jong*

A mother is not a person to lean
on, but a person to make
leaning unnecessary.

—*Dorothy Canfield Fisher*

$\mathcal{N}$o doubt each one of your children thinks that he or she loves you most, and so do I. . . . For me you are the most beautiful and wonderful person in the whole world; merely the fact that you are alive makes the whole world different. . . .

—*Isak Dinesen,*
in a letter to her mother

I spent hours rummaging through my mother's drawers, dabbing her cologne behind my ears, putting on her rhinestone earrings, reading anniversary cards my father had given her, sifting through the hodgepodge in her pocketbooks. I was hunting for clues about what it was to be a woman. I was searching for some secret I knew she had, but wouldn't willingly share with me.

—*Angela Barron McBride*

I know her face by heart.
Sometimes I think
nothing will break her spell.

Daphne Merkin,
of her mother

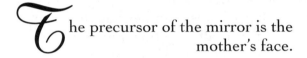

The precursor of the mirror is the
mother's face.

D. W. Winnicott

Mummy herself has told us that she looked upon us more as her friends than her daughters. Now that is all very fine, but still, a friend can't take a mother's place. I need my mother as an example which I can follow.

—*Anne Frank*

$\mathcal{B}$ut what mother and daughter
understand each other, or
even have the sympathy for each other's
lack of understanding?

—*Maya Angelou*

$\mathscr{W}$hen I stopped seeing my
mother with the eyes of
a child, I saw the woman who helped me
give birth to myself.

—*Nancy Friday*

want to lean into her the way
wheat leans into wind.

— *Louise Erdrich,*
of her mother

*A*h, lucky girls who grow up in
the shelter of a mother's
love—a mother who knows how to
contrive opportunities without
conceding favors, how to take advantage
of propinquity without allowing appetite
to be dulled by habit.

—*Edith Wharton*

$\mathcal{D}$ear Mother:
I'm all
right. Stop worrying about me.

*Papyrus letter of seventeen-year-old Egyptian girl,
to her mother, 2000 B.C.*

My mother always found me out. Always. She's been dead for thirty-five years, but I have this feeling that even now she's watching.

—*Natalie Babbitt*

$\mathcal{N}$o matter how old a mother is she watches her middle-aged children for signs of improvement.

—*Florida Scott Maxwell*

[*T*his is to explain] just how
your mom turned
out to be the kind of hairpin she is.

— *Carol Burnett,*
in a note to her daughters

Sure I love the dear silver that
shines in your hair,
And the brow that's all furrowed, and
wrinkled with care.
I kiss the dear fingers, so toil worn for
me,
Oh, God bless you and keep you,
Mother Machree.

—*Rida Johnson Young*

She knew how to make virtues out
of necessities.

—*Audre Lorde,*
of her mother

*W*hatever success comes to me
seems incomplete because
you are so often not at my side to be
glad with me.

—*Helen Keller,*
to her mother

*W*hat do girls *do* who haven't
any mothers to help them
through their troubles?

—*Louisa May Alcott*

I hid myself inside myself, I only considered myself and quietly wrote down all my joys, sorrows and contempt in my diary. . . . I used to be furious with Mummy, and still am sometimes. It's true that she doesn't understand me, but I don't understand her either.

—*Anne Frank*

$\mathcal{M}$y mother will never admit it, but I've always been a disappointment to her. Deep down inside, she'll never forgive herself for giving birth to a daughter who refuses to launder aluminum foil and use it over again.

—*Erma Bombeck*

*W*henever I'm with my mother,
I feel as though I have to
spend the whole time avoiding land
mines.

—*Amy Tan*

*A*cknowledging the tension, distance, and conflict, where is a map of the nurturance, the connection, the ways in which the torch is passed from mother to daughter or from daughter to mother?

—*Louise Bernikow*

*B*laming mother is just a
negative way of
clinging to her still.

—*Nancy Friday*

$\mathcal{Y}$es, Mother. . . . I can see you
are flawed. You have not
hidden it. That is your
greatest gift to me.

—*Alice Walker*

*T*his story is about a woman who loved in spite of starting with the worst possible odds against this fundamental experience, a woman who might have become a creature with a heart of stone.

—*Margaret Truman,*
in the introduction to her biography of her mother

$\mathcal{F}$orgive my own talk of hurt and sorrow. I love you so and only wish I could be home to help you in yours.

— *Sylvia Plath,*
in a letter to her mother

*E*ven if I say my mother was mean, I still love her and anyhow she wasn't that mean. I exaggerate everything I fear.

—*Anne Sexton,*
to her daughter

$\mathcal{M}$y mother is a woman who
speaks with her life as
much as with her tongue.

—*Kesaya E. Noda*

$\mathcal{T}$he woman who bore me is no longer alive, but I seem to be her daughter in increasingly profound ways.

—*Johnnetta B. Cole*

The longer one lives in this hard world motherless, the more a mother's loss makes itself felt.

—*Jane Welsh Carlyle*

$\mathcal{M}$y mother was dead for five years before I knew that I had loved her very much.

—*Lillian Hellman*

She could say "I love you" better than anyone I know . . . [but] I take some small comfort today in knowing that Mother will not insult anyone or embarrass the family. She was responsible for the most excruciating moments of my life.

—*Janet Reno,*
in a eulogy for her mother

*S*he tried in every way to understand me, and she succeeded. It was this deep, loving understanding as long as she lived that more than anything else helped and sustained me on my way to success.

—*Mae West,*
of her mother

*I*t was my mother who fought. Fought! To keep me up to par! To make me study and improve. Fought! To keep my name in the large type she thought I merited. Fought for heat in trains to protect my health. Fought to make ends meet, when each week she had finished sending money to the many dependents that automatically arrived on the high heels of success. Invincible! best describes her.

—*Elsie Janis*

. . . and a

Father

A father is always making his
baby into a little woman.
And when she is a woman he turns her
back again.

—*Enid Bagnold*

*A*ll the feeling which my father could not put into words was in his hand—any dog, child or horse would recognize the kindness of it.

—*Freya Stark*

*T*he thing to remember about
fathers is, they're men.
A girl has to keep it in mind:
They are dragon-seekers, bent on
improbable rescues.
Scratch any father, you find
Someone chock-full of qualms and
romantic terrors,
Believing change is a threat—
Like your first shoes with heels on, like
your first bicycle
It took such months to get.

—*Phyllis McGinley*

$\mathcal{H}$e was generous with his affection, given to great, awkward, engulfing hugs, and I can remember so clearly the smell of his hugs, all starched shirt, tobacco, Old Spice and Cutty Sark. Sometimes I think I've never been properly hugged since.

—*Linda Ellerbee*

It was the schooner Hesperus,
   That sailed the wintry sea;
And the skipper had taken his little
   daughter,
   To bear him company.

—*Henry Wadsworth Longfellow*

$\mathcal{W}$hen it comes to little girls,
God the father has
nothing on father, the god. It's an
awesome responsibility.

—*Frank Pittman*

$\mathcal{C}$hildren want to feel instinctively
that their father is behind them
as solid as a mountain, but, like a
mountain, is something to look up to.

—*Dorothy Thompson*

$\mathcal{Y}$our father's upstairs. You can
call him "Mr. President"
now.

—*Maude Shaw,*
to Caroline Kennedy after her father's election

*W*henever I try to recall that
long-ago first day at
school only one memory shines through:
my father held my hand.

—*Marcelene Cox*

$\mathcal{I}$t was my father's hand that
opened wide
The door to poetry, where the printed
line
Became alive.

—Helen Bean Byerly

$\mathcal{W}$omen's childhood
relationships
with their fathers are important to them
all their lives.

—*Stella Chess*

$\mathcal{M}$y heart is happy, my mind is
free
I had a father who talked with me.

—*Hilda Bigelow*

*F*athers represent another way of
looking at life—the possibility
of an alternative dialogue.

—*Louise J. Kaplan*

*Y*ou teach your daughters the diameters of the planets, and wonder what you have done that they do not delight in your company.

—*Samuel Johnson*

The father of a daughter is nothing but a high-class hostage. A father turns a stony face to his sons, berates them, shakes his antlers, paws the ground, snorts, runs them into the underbrush, but when his daughter puts her arm over his shoulder and says, "Daddy, I need to ask you something," he is a pat of butter in a hot frying pan.

— *Garrison Keillor*

A daughter needs a loving,
available,
predictable father. . . .

— *Victoria Secunda*

*H*e opened the jar of pickles
when no one else could.
He was the only one in the house who
wasn't afraid to go in the basement by
himself. He cut himself shaving, but no
one kissed it or got excited about it. It
was understood when it rained, he got
the car and brought it around to the
door. When anyone was sick, he went
out to get the prescription filled. He
took lots of pictures . . . but he was
never in them.

— *Erma Bombeck, of her father*

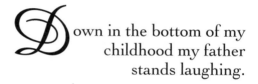

$\mathcal{D}$own in the bottom of my
childhood my father
stands laughing.

— *Tove Ditlevsen*

$\mathcal{N}$o music is so pleasant to my ears as that word—father.

—*Lydia Maria Child*

$\mathcal{B}$e kind to thy father, for when
thou wert young,
Who loved thee so fondly as he?
He caught the first accents that fell from
thy tongue,
And joined in thy innocent glee.

—*Margaret Courtney*

$\mathcal{F}$athers embody a delicious mixture
of familiarity and novelty. They
are novel without being strange or
frightening.

—*Louise J. Kaplan*

$\mathcal{E}$very time I'm about to go to bed with a guy, I have to look at my Dad's name all over the guy's underwear.

—*Marci Klein*

$\mathcal{M}$ost fathers don't see the war within the daughter, her struggles with conflicting images of the idealized and flawed father. . . .

— *Victoria Secunda*

Certain it is that there is no kind of affection so purely angelic as that of a father for a daughter. He beholds both with and without regard to her sex. In love to our wives there is desire; to our sons there is ambition; but in that to our daughters there is something which there are no words to express.

—Joseph Addison

*F*our people, four lives that boiled
down to one life and that was
my father's. What occupied him was
what occupied us.

— *Irene Mayer Selznick*

*H*er Father was waiting. When she saw him, she felt the usual shift in her feelings. A lift, a jump, a tug. Pleasure, but not totally. Love, but not completely. Dependence. Fear, familiarity, identification. That's part of me there, walking along. Tree from which I sprang. His spasm produced me. A shake of his body and here I am. . . .

—*Shirley Anne Graw*

I wanted him to cherish and approve of me, not as he had when I was a child, but as the woman I was, who had her own mind and made her own choices.

—*Adrienne Rich*

$\mathcal{I}$ want something from Daddy that he is not able to give me. . . . It is only that I long for Daddy's real love: not only as his child, but for me — Anne, myself.

—Anne Frank

$\mathcal{Y}$ou appear to me so superior, so elevated above other men; I contemplate you with such strange mixture of humility, admiration, reverence, love and pride, that very little superstition would be necessary to make me worship you as a superior being. . . . I had rather not live than not be the daughter of such a man.

— *Theodosia Burr,*
in a letter to her father Aaron

*H*e sometimes forgets that he is Caesar, but I always remember that I am Caesar's daughter.

—*Julia,*
daughter of the Roman emperor Augustus

A doting father is not simply surprised when his little girl grows up, he is crushed.

— *Victoria Secunda*

*H*aply when I shall wed,
That lord whose hand
must take my plight shall carry
Half my love with him, half my care,
and duty.
Sure I shall never marry like my sisters,
To love my father all.

— *William Shakespeare,*
from a speech by Cordelia to her father, King Lear

*J*t isn't that I'm a weak father, it's just that she's a strong daughter!

—Henry Fonda,
of his daughter Jane

*M*y father . . . lived as if he were poured from iron, and loved his family with a vulnerability that was touching.

—*Mari E. Evans*

*H*appy is it to place a daughter;
yet it pains a father's heart
when he delivers to another's house a
child, the object of his tender care.

—*Euripides*

The meaningful role of the father of the bride was played out long before the church music began. It stretched across those years of infancy and puberty, adolescence and young adulthood. That's when she needs you at her side.

— *Tom Brokaw*

$\mathcal{B}$eing a father
Is quite a
bother
You improve them mentally
And straighten them dentally,
But after you've raised them and
educated them and
gowned them
They take their little fingers
and wrap you around
them.

—*Ogden Nash*

$\mathcal{M}$y father walked with me, and
still does walk,
Yet now, he reckons neither time nor
space.

—*Mary Salinda Foster*

$\mathcal{I}$t's only when you grow up and
step back from him, or leave
him for your own career and your own
home — it's only then that you can
measure his greatness and fully
appreciate it. Pride reinforces love.

*—Margaret Truman
of her father Harry*

To a father waxing old nothing is dearer than a daughter; sons have spirits of a higher pitch, but less inclined to sweet, endearing tenderness.

—*Euripides*

$\mathcal{M}$y dear father! When I
remember him, it is
always with his arms open wide to love
and comfort me.

—*Isobel Field*

*M*y father died
many years
ago,
and yet when something special
happens to me,
I talk to him secretly
not really knowing
whether he hears,
but it makes me feel better
to half believe it.

—*Nataha Josefowitz*

*I*t doesn't matter who my father
was; it matters who I
remember he was.

—*Anne Sexton*

$\mathcal{F}$ather. I write all my poems so I
may bury you more kindly.
Father. I write all my poems to keep you
alive.

—*Deborah Keenan*

*L*ike all children I had taken my father for granted. Now that I had lost him, I felt an emptiness that could never be filled. But I did not let myself cry, believing as a Muslim that tears pull a spirit earthward and won't let it be free.

— *Benazir Bhutto*

One day I found in my hands the manuscript of a poem in my father's handwriting. He had died when I was only fifteen. We had been in love with each other since I could remember, but he had died while our minds were still separated by my immaturity.

—*Katherine Butler Hathaway*

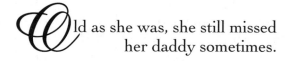

*O*ld as she was, she still missed
her daddy sometimes.

—Gloria Naylor

There is something like a line of gold thread running through the man's words when he talks to his daughter, and gradually over the years it gets to be long enough for you to pick up in your hands and weave into a cloth that feels like love itself.

—*John Gregory Brown*

The history, the root, the strength
of my father is the strength we
now rest on.

—*Carolyn M. Rodgers*

$\mathcal{M}$y father's gifts . . . are daily surprises: my love of naturalness, the tone of my voice, my very face, eyes, and hair.

—*Alice Walker*

Parents

$\mathcal{I}$n the next year or so, my signature will appear on $60 billion of United States currency. More important to me, however, is the signature that appears on my life—the strong, proud, assertive handwriting of a loving father and mother.

—*Katherine D. Ortega*

$\mathcal{M}$y father got me strong and
straight and slim
And I give thanks to him.
My mother bore me glad and sound and
sweet,
I kiss her feet!

—*Marguerite Wilkinson*

$\mathcal{W}$e all carry the Houses of our
Youth inside, and our
Parents, too, grown small enough to fit
within our Hearts.

—*Erica Jong*

She did not understand how her
father could have reached
such age and eminence without learning
that all mothers are as infallible as any
pope and more righteous than any saint.

—*Frances Newman*

*O*ne remembers different persons differently, some by the impact they have made on our emotions, and others by the impression they leave in our minds.

—*Hallie Burnett*

W omen know
The way to
rear up children (to be just),
They know a merry, simple, tender
knack
Of tying sashes, fitting babies' shoes,
And stringing pretty words that make
no sense,
And kissing full sense into empty words;
Which things are corals to cut life upon
Although such trifles.

—*Elizabeth Barrett Browning*

*O*ur father presents an optional
set of rhythms and responses
for us to connect to. As a second home
base, he makes it safer to roam. With
him as an ally—a love—it is safer, too,
to show that we're mad when we're mad
at our mother. We can hate and not be
abandoned, hate and still love.

—*Judith Viorst*

$\mathcal{I}$ was feeling like the center of a wheel with two spokes missing. Then those two spokes were put into place and all of a sudden the wobble was gone.

—*Karen Tashjian,*
on finding her biological parents

They shared decisions and the making of all policy, both in their business and in the family. . . . They spoke all through my childhood with one unfragmentable and unappealable voice.

—*Audre Lorde,*
of her parents

The thing that impresses me the most about Americans is the way parents obey their children.

—*King Edward VIII*

*D*id you ever meet a mother who complained that her child phoned her too often? Me neither.

—*Maureen Lipman*

$\mathcal{F}$rom this day you must be a
stranger to one of your
parents. Your mother will never see you
again if you do *not* marry Mr. Collins,
and I will never see you again if you *do*.

—*Jane Austen*

They were always reading the
law to her at home, which
might not have been so bad if her father
and mother had read from the
same book.

—*Jessamyn West*

$\mathcal{H}$ere is the beginning of understanding: most parents are doing their best, and most children are doing their best, and they're doing pretty well, all things considered.

—*Richard Louv*

$\mathcal{M}$ost parents don't worry about a daughter until she fails to show up for breakfast. Then it's too late.

—*Frank McKinnley Hubbard*

A father is available to help his daughter balance both her love and her anger toward her mother, to moderate the inevitable emotional extremes in the intense mother-daughter equation.

— *Victoria Secunda*

You never get over bein' a child
long's you have a mother to
go to.

—*Sarah Orne Jewett*

*P*arenting is not logical. If it were, we would never have to read a book, never need a family therapist, and never feel the urge to call a close friend late at night for support after a particularly trying bedtime scene. . . . We have moments of logic, but life is run by a much larger force. Life is filled with disagreement, opposition, illusion, irrational thinking, miracle, meaning, surprise, and wonder.

Jeanne Elium and Don Elium, Raising a Daughter

*M*y parents waited ten years for me; that's the way they always put it, as if I were a late train to a place they desperately wanted to go.

—*Kitty Burns Florey*

$\mathcal{I}$t is not a bad thing that children should occasionally, and politely, put parents in their place.

—*Colette*

When a mother—as fond mothers often will—vows she knows every thought in her daughter's heart, I think she pretends to know a great deal too much; nor can there be a wholesomer task for the elders, as our young subjects grow up, naturally demanding liberty and citizens' rights, than for us to gracefully abdicate our sovereign pretensions and claims of absolute control.

—*William Makepeace Thackeray*

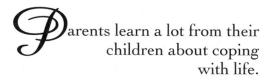

*P*arents learn a lot from their
children about coping
with life.

—*Muriel Spark*

he death of any loved parent is an incalculable lasting blow. Because no one ever loves you again like that.

—Brenda Ueland

The debt of gratitude we owe our mother and father goes forward, not backward. What we owe our parents is the bill presented to us by our children.

—*Nancy Friday*

The
Family
Face

$\mathcal{T}$he family is like a book—the
children are the leaves,
The parents are the covers that
protective beauty gives.
At first the pages of the book are blank
and purely fair,
But time soon writeth memories and
painteth pictures there.
Love is the little golden clasp that
bindeth up the trust,
Oh, break it not, lest all the leaves shall
scatter and be lost.

—*Anonymous*

*T*here is no such thing as Society.
There are individual men and
women, and there are families.

—*Margaret Thatcher*

$\mathcal{H}$ow many different things a family can be — a nest of tenderness, a jail of the heart, a nursery of souls.

— *George Howe Colt*

*G*iving up her home had been a much greater wrench than she had expected. . . . She had a curious sense of her own roots twined around the house, as she had once seen a tree's roots around an old shrine. In time the roots had grown into every crevice until shrine and tree were one indestructible entity.

—Alice Tisdale Hobart

$\mathcal{H}$ome is the place where, when
you have to go there, they
have to take you in.

—*Robert Frost*

Family values are a little like family vacations—subject to changeable weather and remembered more fondly with the passage of time. Though it rained all week at the beach, it's often the momentary rainbows that we remember.

—*Leslie Dryfous*

$\mathcal{A}$ll daughters, even the most aggravated by their mothers, have a secret respect for them. They believe perhaps that they can do everything better than their mothers can, and many things they *can* do better, but they have not yet lived long enough to be sure how successfully they will meet the major emergencies of life, which lie, sometimes quite creditably, *behind* their mothers.

—*Phyllis Bottane*

Families name us and define us, give us strength, give us grief. All our lives we struggle to embrace or escape their influence. They are magnets that both hold us close and drive us away.

—*George Howe Colt*

*F*amily life! The United Nations is child's play compared to the tugs and splits and need to understand and forgive in any family.

—*May Sarton*

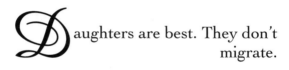

*D*aughters are best. They don't
migrate.

—*Alan Bennett*

have always enjoyed one great
blessing in life, *viz:* the fullest
sympathy of my own family.

—*Elizabeth Blackwell, in a*
letter to her daughter

Soup is a lot like a family. Each ingredient enhances the others; each batch has its own characteristics; and it needs time to simmer to reach full flavor.

—*Marge Kennedy*

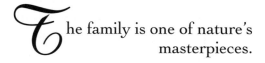

The family is one of nature's
masterpieces.

—*George Santayana*

[*F*amily] bonds are formed less by moments of celebration and of crisis than by the quiet, undramatic accretion of minutiae — the remark on the way out the door, the chore undone, the unexpected smile.

— George Howe Colt

$\mathcal{F}$amily is just an accident. . . . They don't mean to get on your nerves. They don't even mean to be your family, they just are. . . .

—*Marsha Norman*

A daughter is a mother's gender partner, her closest ally in the family confederacy, an extension of her self. And mothers are their daughters' role model, their biological and emotional road map, the arbiter of all their relationships.

—*Victoria Secunda*

$\mathcal{C}$all it a clan, call it a network, call
it a tribe, call it a family.
Whatever you call it, whoever you are,
you need one.

—*Jane Howard*

*W*henever we were on a plane
we had a family.

*—Liza Minnelli,
on life with her mother, Judy Garland, and her
father, Vincent Minnelli*

*W*hat families have in common
the world around is that
they are the place where people learn
who they are and how to
be that way. . . .

—*Jean Illsley Clark*

Families will not be broken. Curse and expel them, send their children wandering, drown them in flood and fires, and old women will make songs out of all these sorrows and sit on the porches and sing them on mild evenings.

—*Marilynne Robinson*

$\mathcal{T}$he family—that dear octopus
from whose tentacles we
never quite escape, nor, in our inmost
hearts, ever quite wish to.

—*Dodie Smith*

$\mathcal{S}$ometimes I need to let you know
how beautiful you are to me—
all of you—and how much pride I feel in
you. And so I come to my private
sanctuary and record a moment in time,
a moment when you were elsewhere and
I needed to share with you.

—*Isa Kogon, to her daughters*

The informality of family life is a blessed condition that allows us to become our best while looking our worst.

—*Marge Kennedy*

"*Flowers o' the home,*" says he,
"*Are daughters.*"

—*Marceline Desbordes-Valmore*

$\mathcal{I}$f the family were a fruit, it would
be an orange, a circle of sections,
held together but separable—each
segment distinct.

—*Letty Cottin Pogrebin*

$\mathcal{I}$f the family were a building, it would be an old but solid structure that contains human history, and appeals to those who see the carved moldings under all the plaster, the wide plank floors under the linoleum, the possibilities.

—*Letty Cottin Pogrebin*

$\mathcal{L}$ike all cultures, one of the family's first jobs is to persuade its members they're special. . . . The persuasion consists of stories showing family members demonstrating admirable traits, which it claims are family traits. Attention to the stories' actual truth is never the family's most compelling consideration. Encouraging belief is. The family survival depends on the shared sensibility of its members.

—*Elizabeth Stone*

*W*ithin our family there was no such thing as a person who did not matter. Second cousins thrice removed mattered. We knew—and thriftily made use of—everybody's middle name. We knew who was buried where. We all mattered, and the dead most of all.

—*Shirley Abbott*

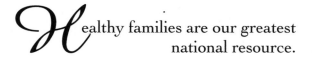

*H*ealthy families are our greatest
national resource.

—*Dolores Curran*

$\mathcal{I}$n families there are matters of which none speaks, or even alludes. There are no words for these matters, as the binding skeleton beneath the flesh is never acknowledged by us and, when at last it defines itself, is after all an obscenity.

—*Joyce Carol Oates*

$\mathcal{I}$n some families, *please* is described as the magic word. In our house, however, it was *sorry*.

—*Margaret Laurence*

[Our family is] a wonderfully messy arrangement, in which relationships overlap, underlie, support, and oppose one another. . . . It has held together, often out of shared memories and hopes, sometimes out of the lure of my sisters' cooking, and sometimes out of sheer stubbornness. And like the world itself, our family is renewed by each baby.

—*Marge Kennedy*

*H*ome, as far as I'm concerned,
is the place you have to
leave. And then, if you're like me, spend
the rest of your life mourning.

—*Paulette Bates Aden*

There is nothing like staying at home for real comfort.

—*Jane Austen*

$\mathcal{W}$e are born into them, marry into them, even create them among the people we love. They come large and extended . . . or small and nuclear. But whatever their size or wherever they live, strong families give us the nurturance and strength we need in order to survive.

—*Andrea Davis*

$\mathcal{F}$amilies are the most beautiful
things in all the world.

—*Louisa May Alcott*

$\mathcal{H}$appy or unhappy, families are all mysterious. We have only to imagine how differently we would be described—and will be, after our deaths—by each of the family members who believe they know us.

—*Gloria Steinem*

I am the family face;
Flesh perishes, I
live on,
Projecting trait and trace
Through time to times anon,
And leaping from place to place
Over oblivion.

—*Thomas Hardy*

The Root
of the
Heart

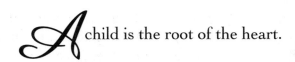

$\mathcal{A}$ child is the root of the heart.

—*Carolina Maria de Jesús*

*W*hen a child enters the world
through you, it alters
everything on a psychic, psychological
and purely practical level.

—*Jane Fonda*

*L*ife is the first gift, love the
second, and
understanding the third.

—*Marge Piercy*

To me the only answer a woman can make to the destructive forces of the world is creation. And the most ecstatic form of creation is the creation of new life.

—*Jessie Bernard,*
written to her unborn daughter

$\mathscr{P}$robably there is nothing in human nature more resonant with charges than the flow of energy between two biologically alike bodies, one of which has lain in amniotic bliss inside the other, one which has labored to give birth to the other.

—*Adrienne Rich*

I think a parent is always tougher on a child of the same sex—because they're *us*. Vanessa is exactly me: stubborn, independent-minded, emotional, quixotic, moody—and lacking in confidence.

—*Jane Fonda*

$\mathcal{I}$t seems to me that since I've had children, I've grown richer and deeper. They may have slowed down my writing for a while, but when I did write, I had more of a self to speak from.

—*Anne Tyler*

When I had my daughter, I learned what the sound of one hand clapping is—it's a woman holding an infant in one arm and a pen in the other.

—*Kate Braverman*

*W*e can't form our children on our own concepts; we must take them and love them as God gives them to us.

—*Johann Wolfgang von Goethe*

*Y*ou may give them your love
but not your thoughts.
For they have their own
thoughts.
You may house their bodies but not
their souls,
For their souls dwell in the house of
tomorrow,
which you cannot visit, not even in your
dreams.

—*Kahlil Gibran*

We have seen that men are learning that work, productivity, and marriage may be very important parts of life, but they are not its whole cloth. The rest of the fabric is made of nurturing relationships, especially those with children — relationships which are intimate, trusting, humane, complex, and full of care.

—*Kyle D. Pruett*

$\mathcal{W}$e have to give ourselves—men in particular—permission to really be with and get to know our children.

—*Anonymous*

$\mathcal{S}$he discovered with great delight
that one does not love one's
children just because they are one's
children but because of the friendship
formed while raising them.

— *Gabriel García Márquez*

Children aren't happy with
nothing to ignore,
And that's what parents were
created for.

—*Ogden Nash*

$\mathscr{C}$hildren have never been very
good at listening to their
elders, but they have never failed to
imitate them.

—*James Baldwin*

*E*ach child is an adventure into a better life—an opportunity to change the old pattern and make it new.

—Hubert H. Humphrey

$\mathcal{W}$hen the voices of children are
heard on the green,
And laughing is heard on the hill,
My heart is at rest within my breast,
And everything else is still.

— *William Blake*

$\mathcal{W}$hat a difference it makes to
come home to a child!

—*Margaret Fuller*

$\mathcal{M}$others for miles around worried about Zuckerman's swing. They feared some child would fall off. But no child ever did. Children almost always hang onto things tighter than their parents think they will.

—*E. B. White*

*C*hildren when they are little make
parents fools; when they are
great they make them mad.

— *George Herbert*

*C*hildren can be awe-inspiringly horrible; manipulative, aggressive, rude, and unfeeling to a point where I often think that, if armed, they would make up the most terrifying force the world has ever seen.

—*Jill Tweedie*

What children expect from grownups is not to be "understood," but only to be loved, even though this love may be expressed clumsily or in sternness. Intimacy does not exist between generations —only trust.

—Carl Zucker

$\mathcal{B}$etween the dark and the daylight,
When the night is beginning to lower,
Comes a pause in the day's occupations,
That is known as the Children's Hour.

—*Henry Wadsworth Longfellow*

*W*e find delight in the beauty
and happiness of children
that makes the heart too big for
the body.

—*Ralph Waldo Emerson*

*Crossing the street,
I saw the parents
and the child
At their window, gleaming with fruit
With evening's mild gold leaf.*

—*James Ingram Merrill*

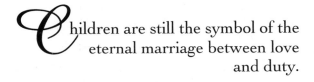

Children are still the symbol of the eternal marriage between love and duty.

—*George Eliot*

There's only one pretty child in the world, and every mother has it.

—*J. C. Bridge*

*L*ittle girls are the nicest things that happen to people. They are born with a little bit of angelshine about them and though it wears thin sometimes there is always enough left to lasso your heart—even when they are sitting in the mud, or crying temperamental tears, or parading up the street in their mother's best clothes.

—*Alan Beck*

$\mathcal{A}$ child is a quicksilver fountain
spilling over with tomorrows
and tomorrows
and that is why
she is richer than you and I.

— *Tom Bradley*

There is always one moment in childhood when the door opens and lets the future in.

—*Graham Greene*

$\mathscr{I}$ wasn't used to children and they were getting on my nerves. Worse, it appeared that I was a child, too. I hadn't known that before; I though I was just short.

—*Florence King,*
on her first day in kindergarten

$\mathcal{M}$y children have taught me things. Things I thought I knew. The most profound wisdom they have given me is a respect for human vulnerability. I have known people are resilient, but I didn't appreciate how fragile they are. Until children learn to hide their feelings, you read them in their faces, gestures, and postures. The sheer visibility of shyness, pain, and rejection let me recognize and remember them.

—*Shirley Nelson Garner*

I have found the best way to give advice to your children is to find out what they want and then advise them to do it.

—*Harry S. Truman*

Children and fools want everything, because they want wit to distinguish; there is no stronger evidence of a crazy understanding than in the making too large of a catalogue of things necessary.

—George Savile,
Marquess of Halifax, Advice to a Daughter

*S*ecrets are kept from children, a lid on top of the soup kettle, so they don't boil over with too much truth.

—*Amy Tan*

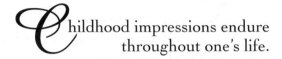

*C*hildhood impressions endure
throughout one's life.

— *William Hatie*

$\mathcal{T}$o grown people a girl of fifteen
and a half is a child still; to
herself she is very old and very real,
perhaps, than ever before or after. . . .

—*Margaret Widdemer*

The best way to keep children at home is to make it pleasant — and let the air out of the tires.

—*Dorothy Parker*

$\mathcal{G}$rown don't mean nothing to a
mother. A child is a child.
They get bigger, older, but not
grown. In my heart it doesn't
mean a thing.

— *Toni Morrison*

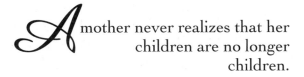

A mother never realizes that her children are no longer children.

—*Holbrook Jackson*

$\mathcal{L}$et your children go if you want
to keep them.

—*Malcolm Forbes*

$\mathcal{H}$ome can never be transferred;
never repeated in the
experience of an individual. The place
consecrated by paternal love, by the
innocence and sports of childhood, by
the first acquaintance with nature; by
the linking of the heart to the visible
creation, is the only home.

—*C. M. Sedgwick*

Our daughters and sons have
burst
from the marionette show
leaving a tangle of strings
and gone into the unlit audience.

—*Maxine Kumin*

*W*hen she had been a child, children were expected to defer to their parents in everything, to wait on them and help them around the house and so on; but when she became a parent and was ready to enjoy her turn at being deferred to, the winds of fashion in child rearing had changed, and parents were expected to defer to their children in hopes of not squelching their imagination and creativity. She had missed out all the way around.

—*Lisa Alther*

$\mathcal{A}$ll my children have spoken
for themselves since they
first learned to speak and not always
with my advance approval and I expect
that to continue in the future.

— *Gerald Ford*

There are only two lasting bequests we can hope to give our children. One of these is roots, the other, wings.

—*Hodding Carter*

Life

$\mathcal{Y}$our children are not your
children.
They are the sons and
daughters Life's longing for itself.

—*Kahlil Gabran*

*W*hat I most wanted for my daughter was that she be able to soar confidently *in her own sky*, wherever that might be, and if there was space for me as well I would, indeed, have reaped what I had tried to sow.

—*Helen Claes*

Suddenly, through birthing a daughter, a woman finds herself face to face not only with an infant, a little girl, a woman-to-be, but also with her own unresolved conflicts from the past and her hopes and dreams for the future. . . .

—*Elizabeth Debold,*
Idelisse Malave, and Marie Wilson

$\mathcal{M}$y mother groan'd, my father
wept,
Into the dangerous world I leapt;
Helpless, naked, piping loud,
Like a fiend hid in a cloud.

— *William Blake*

*I*n peasant communities where things didn't change and where people died in the beds they were born in, grandparents taught the young what the end of life was going to be. So you looked at your mother, if you were a girl, and learned what it was like to be a bride, a young mother. Then you looked at your grandmother and you knew what it was like to be old. Children . . . were prepared for the end of life at the beginning.

—*Margaret Mead*

*L*ife would shape her, not me.
All we were good for was to
make the introductions.

—*Helen Hayes,*
of her daughter

*G*od speed you on your errand
of mercy, my own dearest
child. . . .I do not ask you
to spare yourself for your own
sake, but for the sake of the cause.

—*Fanny Nightingale,*
in a letter to her daughter, Florence

*A*s I watched her at play . . . it came to me that this child would pass through life as the angels live in Heaven. The difficulties of existence would never be hers.

—*Pearl S. Buck,*
of her mentally retarded daughter

*A*dolescence is that time
between pigtails and
cocktails.

—*Anonymous*

Oh, for those young embroiderers of bygone days, sitting on a hard little stool in the shelter of their mother's ample skirts! Maternal authority kept them there for years and years, never rising except to change the skein of silk or to elope with a stranger.

— *Colette*

$\mathcal{F}$or after all, that is what I am striving for more than anything else in the world—to be a great soul; to experience life so fully that I shall be able to understand the joys, the aspirations, the defeat, the struggle, the discouragements of those around me.

—*Lella Secor,*
in a letter to her mother

*L*ove and grief and motherhood,
    Fame and mirth and scorn—
These are all shall befall
    Any woman born.

—*Margaret Widdemer*

$\mathcal{I}$f I had another child—I'd like a girl—I can't say just how I'd raise her, but one thing I can tell you is that she will not be spoiled. The whole thing is about earning your own way and you don't really get there until you earn it. That's the real truth.

— *Tina Turner*

I stopped believing in Santa Claus when I was six. Mother took me to see him in a department store and he asked me for my autograph.

—*Shirley Temple*

I hope I showed you that loving means letting go too. Letting go of NEEDING to be loved, and simply loving. It's somewhat like the way you girls tend your plants. Their response is born of your initial actions. Love blooms that way too. When we love, we become loved.

—*Isa Kogon,*
to her daughters

*D*on't be in a hurry, Miranda . . .
the old mother, you know
remembers herself at your age,
sixteen is it, well I,
Well you are too beautiful, time
to leave . . . ?

—*Judith Kazantzis,
in "For My Daughter"*

$\mathcal{I}$ pray that I may be all that she would have been had she lived in an age when women could aspire and achieve and daughters [were] cherished as much as sons.

—*Ruth Bader Ginsburg,*
of her mother

There is a point where you aren't
as much a mom and a daughter
as you are adults and friends.

—*Jamie Lee Curtis*

[*My* mother told me:] "You must decide whether you want to get married someday, or have a career." . . . I set my sights on the career. I thought, what does any man really have to offer me?

—*Annie Elizabeth Delany*

I thought about all of us women and how we spend half our lives rebelling against our mothers and the next half rebelling against our daughters.

—*Lois Wyse*

If you go away from your own place and people—the place you spent your childhood in, all your life you'll be sick with home sickness and you'll never have a home. You can find a better place, perhaps, a way of life you like better, but *home* is gone out of your heart, and you'll be hunting it all your life long.

—*Agnes Smedley*

*M*other, I long to get married
I long to be a bride,
I long to lay by that young man
And close to by his side
Close to by his side
Oh happy I should be,
For I'm young and merry and almost
weary
Of my virginity.

—*Anonymous*

"Oh dear," thought Meg, "married life is very trying, and does need infinite patience, as well as love, as mother says."

—*Louisa May Alcott*

*A*h! I have handed over
The jewel to its
owner;
So from henceforth, my dear pillow,
Let us two sleep together . . .

—Otomo no Sakano-e no Iratsume,
in "On the Marriage of a Daughter"

$\mathcal{W}$e'd have been much better off
. . . putting sandwich boards
on their backs reading "I'm the daughter
of Henry Ford . . . worth this many
million dollars . . . this is my telephone
number."

—*Anne McDonnel Ford,*
of her daughters' failed marriages

My mother accepted Ken as she had never accepted anyone before. It may have been merely exhaustion.

—*Erica Jong,*
of her fourth husband

*T*he ultimate end of your
education was to make
you a good wife.

—*Lady Mary Wortley Montagu,*
in a letter to her daughter

A mother's the hardest to forgive.
Life is the fruit she longs to
hand you,
Ripe on a plate. And while you live,
Relentlessly she understands you.

— *Phyllis McGinley*

*I*t really seems tonight as if I were parting with someone dear — saying good-bye to somebody I loved. In the past few hours I have lived over nearly all of life's struggles, and the most painful is the memory of my mother's long and weary efforts to get her six children up into womanhood and manhood . . . . And yet with it all, I know there was an undercurrent of joy and love which makes the summing-up vastly in their favor.

—*Susan B. Anthony,*
in a letter to her mother

*W*e waken and count our
daughters.
Otherwise, nothing happens.

—*Carolyn Kizer*

$\mathcal{A}$ man is free to go as high as he
can reach up to; but I, with
all my style and pep, can't get a man my
equal because a girl is always judged by
her mother.

—*Anzia Yezierska*

Our mythology tells us so much about fathers and sons. . . . What do we know about mothers and daughters? . . . Our power is so oblique, so hidden, so ethereal a matter, that we rarely struggle with our daughters over actual kingdoms or corporate shares. On the other hand, our attractiveness dries as theirs blooms, our journey shortens as theirs begins. We too must be afraid and awed and amazed that we cannot live forever and that our replacements are eager for their turn, indifferent to our wishes, ready to leave us behind.

—*Anne Roiphe*

am a reflection of my mother's secret poetry as well as of her hidden angers.

—*Audre Lorde*

From the earliest times the old have rubbed it into the young that they are wiser than they, and before the young had discovered what nonsense this was they were old too, and it profited them to carry on the imposture.

— W. Somerset Maugham

$\mathcal{Y}$ou are still and always will be
tops with me.

—*Joseph P. Kennedy,*
to his daughter Kathleen on her marriage

$\mathcal{S}$he was life itself to me. Whenever I asked myself what life was for or what the meaning of life was, I needed only to look over at her or call her if I was away. . . . or in the last days reach over and hold her old gnarled hand, to know the answer.

—*Janet Reno,*
of her mother

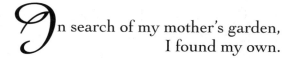

$\mathcal{I}$n search of my mother's garden,
I found my own.

—*Alice Walker*

To be rooted is probably the most important and least recognized need of the human soul.

—*Simone Weil*

$\mathcal{I}$ . . . have another cup of coffee
with my mother. We get
along very well, veterans of a guerrilla
war we never understood.

—*Joan Didion*

*M*other who gave me life
I think of women
bearing
women. Forgive me the wisdom
I would not learn from you.

— *Gwen Harwood*

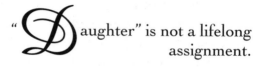

" **D**aughter" is not a lifelong
assignment.

—*Shirley Abbott*

*N*ow I know what it is to live
and to love life, and really
I should be sorry now to leave life. I
know you will be glad to hear this,
dearest Mum. God has indeed made life
rich in interests and blessings, and I
wish for no other earth, no other world
but this one.

—*Florence Nightingale,*
in a letter to her mother

Words of Wisdom

When you educate a man you educate an individual, but when you educate a woman, you educate a nation.

—*Johnnetta B. Cole*

*H*ere's what I taught my daughters: Become women of substance. Work for yourselves if you can. That way you won't have to take any lip, and you can work the hours you want. Never buy artificial fabric; always buy silk. If you can save any money, buy your own place and keep it in your name. . . . And if you hate to save, or be tied down, put your money in jewelry. . . . And never, never do a job if it isn't fun.

—*Carolyn See*

*K*indness and intelligence don't always deliver us from the pitfalls and traps: there are always failures of love, of will, of imagination. There is no way to take the danger out of human relationships.

—*Barbara Grizzuti Harrison*

*J*ust be yourself, develop
autonomy, don't feel
like you have to be like others; take your
time about developing and all will turn
out well, with only the usual quota of
heartbreaks which are the condition of
mankind.

—*Jessie Bernard,
in a letter to her daughter*

$\mathcal{T}$he generation of daughters now growing up may be the first one in history to feel that motherhood can be a choice among many that a woman can make.

—*Signe Hammer*

One must leave one's parents
early, especially one's
mother. Mothers are never any good for
their daughters. They forget they were
just as ugly and silly and scraggy when
they were little girls.

—*Mrs. Robert Henery*

*L*ord Illingworth: All women become like their mothers. That is their tragedy.
Mrs. Allonby: No man does. That is his.

—*Oscar Wilde*

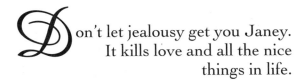

*D*on't let jealousy get you Janey.
It kills love and all the nice
things in life.

—*Calamity Jane,*
in a journal to her daughter

$\mathcal{Y}$ou need only claim the events
of your life to make
yourself yours.

—*Florida Scott-Maxwell*

$\mathcal{H}$appiness is an imaginary
condition, formerly
often attributed by the living to the
dead, now usually attributed by adults
to children, and by children to adults.

— *Thomas Szasz*

Oh it is wonderful—this human nature with its infinite capacity, and unending desire, for joy. Let someone only strike up a common tune on a wheezy street organ . . . there'll be humming and singing here and there—and the little ones will dance their legs off. Isn't it beautiful?

—*Crystal Eastman,*
in a letter to her mother

She has done what she liked and now she must like what she has done.

— *Winston Churchill,*
on the marriage of his daughter

*B*ehold, every one that useth
proverbs shall use this
proverb against thee, saying, As is the
mother, so is her daughter.

—*Ezekiel 1:16*, The Holy Bible

These remarkable women of olden times are like the ancient painted glass — the art of making them is lost; my mother was less than her mother, and I am less than my mother.

—*Harriet Beecher Stowe*

$\mathcal{I}$ guess we are all busy, but one does make time for the really important things in life.

—*Anne Sexton,*
in a letter to her daughter

$\mathcal{M}$y father advised me that life itself was a crap game: it was one of the two lessons I learned as a child. The other was that overturning a rock was apt to reveal a rattlesnake. As lessons go those two seems to hold up, but not to apply.

—*Joan Didion*

$\mathcal{A}$mong the most disheartening
and dangerous of . . .
advisors, you will often find those
closest to you, your dearest friends,
members of your own family, perhaps,
loving, anxious, and knowing nothing
whatever.

—*Minnie Maddern Fiske*

I, woman, i
can no
longer claim
a mother of flesh
a father of marrow
I, Woman must be
the child of myself.

—*Pat Parker*

[*M*y Dear Mother] . . . Why
must a woman be
ignorant?

—*George Sand,
in a letter to her mother*

$\mathcal{Y}$ou cannot make yourself feel
something you do not feel,
but you can make yourself
do right in spite of your feelings. . . .

—*Pearl S. Buck,*
To My Daughters, With Love

$\mathcal{F}$rom birth to eighteen a girl needs good parents. From eighteen to thirty-five, she needs good looks. From thirty-five to fifty-five, good personality. From fifty-five on, she needs good cash. I'm saving my money.

—*Sophie Tucker*

There is a universal truth that I have found in my work. Everybody longs to be loved. And the greatest thing we can do is let somebody know they are loved and capable of loving.

—*Fred Rogers*

$\mathcal{N}$ever grow a wishbone,
daughter, where your
backbone ought to be.

—*Clementine Paddleford*

The longer we live, and the more we think, the higher the value we learn to put on the friendship and tenderness of parents and of friends. Parents we can have but once; and he promises himself too much, who enters life with the expectation of finding many friends.

—*Samuel Johnson*

I only made one comment. It was "Be yourself," and she has continued to be.

Major Ronald Ferguson,
on the marriage of his daughter,
Sarah, to the Duke of York

$\mathcal{M}$y only advice is to stay aware, listen carefully and yell for help if you need it.

—*Judy Blume*

*B*ut, Mother, there are no trials so great as they suffer who neglect or refuse to do what they believe is their duty. . . . ESPECIALLY DO I MEAN TO LABOR FOR THE ELEVATION OF MY SEX. . . . But I will not speak further upon this subject at this time, only to ask that you will not withhold your consent from my doing anything that I think is my duty to do. You will not, will you, Mother?

—*Lucy Stone, in a letter to her mother*

*S*ince we are in the world of the unfinished, the imperfect, let us make the best of its opportunities and enrich ourselves with its faith and hope and love.

—*Annis Ford Eastman,*
to her daughter Crystal

*R*isk! Risk anything! Care no more for the opinion of others, for those voices. Do the hardest thing on earth for you. Act for yourself. Face the truth.

—*Katherine Mansfield*

*I*f you want to sacrifice the admiration of many men for the criticism of one, go ahead and get married.

—*Katherine Houghton Hepburn,*
to her daughter

*T*hink wrongly, if you please, but in all cases think for yourself.

—*Doris Lessing*

$\mathcal{I}$ love you, 40-year-old Linda, and I love what you do, what you find, what you are — Be your own woman. Belong to those you love.

—*Anne Sexton,*
in a letter to her daughter

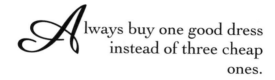

*A*lways buy one good dress instead of three cheap ones.

—*Michele Slung,*
to her daughter

*W*henever I feel myself inferior to everything about me . . . I can still hold up my head and say to myself: . . . "Let me not forget that I am the daughter of a woman who bent her head, trembling, between the blades of a cactus, her wrinkled face full of ecstasy over the promise of a flower, a woman who herself never ceased to flower, untiringly, during three quarters of a century."

—*Colette*

*I*deals and principles are no better than ghosts if they are not incarnated and worked out in people. In loving you I love every high and holy thing—but it isn't truth and justice and loyalty and kindness that I love—it is you. I haven't much faith in anybody's living for the mass—for humanity—without the strong affection for individuals.

—*Annis Ford Eastman,*
to her daughter Crystal

The best thing you can do is believe in yourself. Don't be afraid to try. Don't be afraid to fail. Just try again. Just dust yourself off and try again.

—Judy Green Herbstreit,
to her daughter

$\mathcal{I}$ suppose you think that persons who are as old as your father and myself are always thinking about very grave things, but I know that we are meditating the same old themes that we did when we were ten years old, only we go more gravely about it.

—*Henry David Thoreau,*
in a letter to Ellen Emerson, daughter of
Ralph Waldo Emerson

*E*ach generation's job is to
question what parents
accept as faith, to explore possibilities,
and to adapt the last generation's system
of values for a new age.

—*Frank Pittman*

*Y*ou will do foolish things, but
do them with enthusiasm.

—*Colette,*
to her daughter

The most important thing she'd learned over the years was that there was no way to be a perfect mother and a million ways to be a good one.

—*Jill Churchill*

*B*eing a daughter is only half of the equation; bearing one is the other.

—*Erica Jong*

Bibliography

Robert Andrews, ed. *The Columbia Dictionary of Quotations.* New York: Columbia University Press, 1993.

Tony Augarde, ed. *The Oxford Dictionary of Modern Quotations.* New York: Oxford University Press, 1991.

Maturin M. Ballou, ed. *Notable Thoughts About Women.* Ann Arbor: Gryphon Books, 1971.

John Bartlett. Emily Morrison Beck, ed. *Bartlett's Familiar Quotations.* Boston: Little Brown, 1980.

Gorton Carruth and Eugene Ehrlich, eds. *The Harper Book of American Quotations.* New York: Harper and Row Publishers, 1995.

Stephen Donadio, ed. *The New York Public Library Book of 20th Century American Quotations.* New York: Stonesong Press, 1992.

Bergen Evans, ed. *The Dictionary of Quotation.* New York: Delacorte Press, 1968.

Robert I. Fitzhenry, ed. *The Harper Book of Quotations.* New York: Harper Perennial, 1993.

Max L. Forman, ed. *World's Greatest Quotations.* New York: Exposition Press, 1970.

Robin Hyman, ed. *The Quotation Dictionary.* New York: The MacMillan Company, 1962.

Marjorie P. Katz, ed. *Pegs to Hang Ideas On.* New York: M. Evans and Company, 1973.

Lois L. Kaufman, ed. *To My Daughter.* New York: Peter Pauper Press, 1990.

Alec Lewis, ed. *The Quotable Quotations Book.* New York: Thomas Y. Crowell, 1980.

Illona Linthwaite, ed. *Ain't I a Woman*. New York: Peter Bedrick Books, 1990.

Rosalie Maggio, ed. *The Beacon Book of Quotations by Women*. Boston: Beacon Press, 1992.

Rosalie Maggio, ed. *The New Beacon Book of Quotations by Women*. Boston: Beacon Press, 1996.

Tillie Olsen, ed. *Mother to Daughter, Daughter to Mother, Mothers on Mothering*. Old Westbury: The Feminist Press, 1984.

Elaine Partnow, ed. *The New Quotable Woman*. New York: Facts on File, 1992.

Elaine Partnow, ed. *The Quotable Woman, 1800 - 1981*. New York: Facts on File, 1982.

Karen Payne, ed. *Between Ourselves: Letters Between Mothers and Daughters*. Boston: Houghton Mifflin, 1983.

Lawrence J. Peter, ed. *Peter's Quotations: Ideas for Our Time*. New York: William Morrow, 1977.

Dorothy Winbush Riley, ed. *My Soul Looks Back, 'Less I Forget*. New York: Winbush Publishing, 1991.

W. Safire and L. Safir, eds. *Words of Wisdom*. New York: Simon and Schuster, 1989.

Ned Sherrin, ed. *The Oxford Dictionary of Humorous Quotations*. New York: Oxford University Press, 1995.

William Shakespeare. C. J. Sisson, ed. *William Shakespeare: The Complete Works*. New York: Harper and Row, 1953.

James B. Simpson. *Contemporary Quotations*. New York: Thomas Y. Crowell Co., 1964.

James B. Simpson, comp. *Simpson's Contemporary Quotations*. Boston: Houghton Mifflin, 1988.

James B. Simpson. *Simpson's Contemporary Quotations*. New York: HarperCollins, 1997.

Burton Stevenson, ed. *The Home Book of Quotations Classical and Modern,* 9th Edition. New York: Dodd, Mead & Co., 1958.

Carolyn Warner, ed. *The Last Word: A Treasury of Women's Quotes*. Englewood Cliffs: Prentice-Hall, 1992.

Frank J. Wilstach, ed. *A Dictionary of Similes*. New York: Grosset & Dunlap, 1924.

The MacMillan Dictionary of Quotations. New York: MacMillan Publishing Company, 1989.

Mothers: A Celebration of Love. Philadelphia: The Running Press, 1995.

Motherhood: A Gift of Love. Philadelphia: The Running Press, 1995.